IN THE WINTER OF CITIES

By Tennessee Williams

PLAYS

Battle of Angels
Camino Real
Cat on a Hot Tin Roof
The Eccentricities of a Nightingale
The Glass Menagerie
The Milk Train Doesn't Stop Here Anymore
The Night of the Iguana
Orpheus Descending
Period of Adjustment
The Rose Tattoo
Slapstick Tragedy
A Streetcar Named Desire
Suddenly Last Summer
Summer and Smoke
Sweet Bird of Youth
27 Wagons Full of Cotton

SCREENPLAY

Baby Doll

STORIES

Hard Candy
One Arm

NOVEL

The Roman Spring of Mrs. Stone

In the Winter of Cities

POEMS BY

Tennessee Williams

A New Directions Paperbook

IN MEMORY OF MY GRANDFATHER

The Reverend Walter E. Dakin

(1857-1955)

First published as New Directions Paperbook 154
in 1964.

Second Printing

The author wishes to acknowledge the advice of
William S. Gray in helping him select the poems
included in this volume.

Other poems in this volume first appeared, sometimes
with other titles and in different form, in *Five Young
American Poets* — 1944 (New Directions), *Harper's
Bazaar, Mademoiselle, New Directions 9, 11, 12,*
and *13, Panorama, Partisan Review, Semi-Colon* and
Voices, and are reprinted with the permission of the
publishers.

New Directions Books are published for James
Laughlin by New Directions Publishing Corpora-
tion, 333 Sixth Avenue, New York 10014.

The Contents

Part I

IN JACK-O'-LANTERN'S WEATHER

IN JACK-O'-LANTERN'S WEATHER

I

The marvelous children
          cut their pure ice capers
north of time.
          Being very
          restless expert skaters,
never did they trace
          the same design twice over,

     but each, completed,
had to be detached and lifted clean
on aerial derricks, green
          and boned as swallows.

          None wrote home,
no bulletins were issued of their progress
          which he, the demon,
thought that he could block
with barricades of gold and purple tin foil labeled Fear
and other august titles which they took in their stride,
          leapt over lightly,
always tossing backwards calls of gladness,
that echoed behind them long after they leapt
          and were gone.

II

Much green water, rumorous and vague,
talked of their loss, discussed them in home quarters,
        rolled ghostly tokens shorewards,
corduroy and lawn,
        scraps of song,
            unfinished arithmetic problems,
thumbprints on dog-eared books tossed into corners.
        Mothers' sorrow
        often must be thorned
by soft bird language, earlier than morning,
        snow brought indoors
in exchange for grandmothers' cupboards of linen,
            undignified, flung in every-which-a-direction,
            shouts
that broke windows, orchards festooned
by something wilder than blossoms!

        Oh mothers' sorrow
grievously is pricked by jacks and apples of the earth's
        green-tongued refreshment,
storms that came on without warning, calls, calls,
        running through orchards calling,
        Come home! Come home!
before it gets dreadfully dark and hailstones fall
as big as goose eggs, nearly!
        Stillness. Distance . . .
        A spiral of dust,
            a little upright figure
that bends and twists in curtsies, that does a pavan
        that's stately and gay and capricious,
is stalking about home plate as if he thought he owned it!

Now has begun
        to hum, to whisper
the names of lost ballplayers . . .
the first dark coins of moisture fall on the diamond . . .

        O Mother of Blue Mountain boys,
come to the screen door, calling, *Come home! Come home!*
White milkwagons are hurrying, hurrying down wet
        darkening streets,
                there isn't much time!

        III

I have seen them earlier than morning cross the hall,
        serious-eyed and weighted down by schoolbooks,
as if alarm clocks set at premature hours
had roused them from sleep before it let them go . . .
I have seen their pencil-mark distinctions between this thing
        and that one,
                their blue angles, sharper than gymnastics.
        In Jack-o'-Lantern's weather,
their orderly, schoolteachered troop to the Sunflower River
for an inspection of Flora along those banks
where blacks in white shifts held springtime baptismals,
        Ha, ha! — shouting . . .
                I have seen them
never less than azure-eyed and earnest
        tackle
geometry problems whose Q.E.D.
        is surely speechless wonder . . .

IV

Mothers' sorrow
      grievously is thorned
by shreds of arctic light through dark pine branches,
      halting the morning
with hawk-bone print of heaven.

      The weather, as ever,
is clearing again, with shreds of blue and vapor
      appearing among dark branches . . .
      O Madonna,
aged by unequal sorrows but clothed as ever in silk, blown,
      cherry-printed,
      O singing white enchantress,
I sumon thee now,
      clothed as sorrow is in snow and snow.

TESTA DELL' EFFEBO

Of Flora did his luster spring
and gushing waters bathed him so
that trembling shells were struck and held
until his turning let them go.

Then gold he was when summer was;
unchangeable this turning seemed
and the repose of sculpture told
how thinly gold his shoulder gleamed.

A cloud of birds awoke in him
when Virgo murmured half awake.
Then higher lifted birds and clouds
to break in fire as glasses break.

A lunatic with tranquil eyes
he must have been when he had dimmed
and that town burned wherein was turned
this slender copper cast of him.

CRIED THE FOX

For D.H.L.

I run, cried the fox, in circles
narrower, narrower still,
across the desperate hollow,
skirting the frantic hill

and shall till my brush hangs burning
flame at the hunter's door
continue this fatal returning
to places that failed me before!

Then, with his heart breaking nearly,
the lonely, passionate bark
of the fugitive fox rang out clearly
as bells in the frosty dark,

across the desperate hollow,
skirting the frantic hill,
calling the pack to follow
a prey that escaped them still.

THE EYES

For Oliver

The eyes are last to go out.
They remain long after the face has disappeared regretfully
    into the tissue that it is made of.
The tongue says good-by when the eyes have a lingering
    silence,
for they are the searchers last to abandon the search,
the ones that remain where the drowned have been washed
    ashore,
after the lanterns staying, not saying good-by . . .

The eyes have no faith in that too accessible language.
For them no occasion is simple enough for a word to justify it.
Existence in time, not only their own but ancestral,
encloses all moments in four walls of mirrors.

Closed, they are waiting. Open, they're also waiting.
They are acquainted,
but they have forgotten the name of their acquaintance.

Youth is their uneasy bird, and shadows clearer than light
pass through them at times,
for waters are not more changeable under skies
nor stones under rapids.

The eyes may be steady with that Athenian look
that answers terror with stillness, or they may be quick
with a purely infatuate being. Almost always
the eyes hold onto an image
of someone recently departed or gone a long time ago
or only expected . . .

The eyes are not lucky.
They seem to be hopelessly inclined to linger.

They make additions that come to no final sum.
It is really hard to say if their dark is worse than their light,
their discoveries better or worse than not knowing,

but they are last to go out,
and their going out is always when they are lifted.

FAINT AS LEAF SHADOW

Faint as leaf shadow does he fade
and do you fade in touching him.
And as you fade, the afternoon
fades with you and is cool and dim.

A wall that rises through no space,
division which is shadow-thin,
his eyelids close upon your eyes'
quicksilver which bewilders him.

And then you softly say his name
as though his name upon your tongue
a wall could lift against the drift
of shadow that he fades among.

Sometimes those frontiers of the twain
may seem no longer to exist,
but why, then, is the breath disturbed,
and does the silver body twist,

and why the whisper of a name
as though enquiring, Is it true?
which goes unanswered until sleep
has loosened his fierce hold of you.

THE SIEGE

I build a tottering pillar of my blood
to walk it upright on the tilting street.
The stuff is liquid, it would flow downhill
so very quickly if the hill were steep.

How perilously do these fountains leap
whose reckless voyager along am I!
In mothering darkness, Lord, I pray Thee keep
these springs a single touch of sun could dry.

It is the instant froth that globes the world,
an image gushing in a crimson stream.
But let the crystal break and there would be
the timeless quality but not the dream.

Sometimes I feel the island of my self
a silver mercury that slips and runs,
revolving frantic mirrors in itself
beneath the pressure of a million thumbs.

Then I must that night go in search of one
unknown before but recognized on sight
whose touch, expedient or miracle,
stays panic in me and arrests my flight.

Before day breaks I follow back the street,
companioned, to a rocking space above.
Now do my veins in crimson cabins keep
the wild and witless passengers of love.

All is not lost, they say, all is not lost,
but with the startling knowledge of the blind
their fingers flinch to feel such flimsy walls
against the siege of all that is not I!

THE SOFT CITY

I

Eastward the city with scarcely even a murmur
       turns in the soft dusk,
       the lights of it blur,
       the delicate spires are unequal
as though the emollient dusk had begun to dissolve them . . .

       And the soft air-breathers,
their soft bosoms rising and falling as ferns under water
responding to some impalpably soft pressure,
       turn with the city, too.

       The petals of tenderness in them,
their tentative ways of feeling, not quite reaching out
but ever so gently half reaching out and withdrawing,

withdrawing to where their feminine star is withdrawing,
the planet that turns with them,
       faithfully always and softly . . .

II

And if there is something which is not soft in the city,
such as a cry too hard for the soft mouth to hold,
        God puts a soft stop to it.

Bending invisibly down, He breathes a narcosis
over the panicky face upturned to entreat Him:
a word as soft as *morphine* is the word that God uses,
placing His soft hand over the mouth of the cryer
before it has time to gather the force of a cry.

It is almost as if no cry had ever been thought of . . .

And, yes, over all,
      soft canopy over soft canopy,
          web over soft, soft web,
              gauze hung over gauze,

the mysteries of the tall heaven,
      the tall and very soft heaven,
          are softest of all!

A WREATH FOR
ALEXANDRA MOLOSTVOVA

For Maria Brit-Neva

It is well to remember, to celebrate and remember,
      how as we entered the shadowy vault of
         St. Phillip's,
bearing her roses among us,
      five tall solemn men
in the plain gray clothes of the street,
      burst into song,
and the reverence of candles...

It is well to remember those tall solemn men
      in the clothes they wore on the street,
their faces unweeping but solemn as a departure,
giving her praise as we bore her roses among them,
      and how chill it was till we entered,
and then it was warm, and the reverence of the candles...

It is well to remember, to celebrate and remember
      the chant of her name, Alexandra,
its repetition and the solemnity of it,
      the name Alexandra,
as if an iron bell rang and continued ringing,
      the stately name Alexandra
and again, Alexandra...

It is well to remember the chill of the vault made warm
      by the entrance of roses

23

and the candles' reverence and those tall solemn men
      in the plain gray clothes of the street,
      chanting her name, Alexandra,
the incantation of her name, Alexandra . . .

But it is also well for you to forget,
      little sister, Maria,
to give her peace and forget,
to place in her hands this wreath and a silent white cross
    of Russia
      while saying farewell
and whispering, Sleep, Alexandra . . .

THE BEANSTALK COUNTRY

You know how the mad come into a room,
too boldly,
their eyes exploding on the air like roses,
their entrances from space we never entered.
They're always attended by someone small and friendly
who goes between their awful world and ours
as though explaining but really only smiling,
a snowy gull that dips above a wreck.

They see not us, nor any Sunday caller
among the geraniums and wicker chairs,
for they are Jacks who climb the beanstalk country,
a place of hammers and tremendous beams,
compared to which the glassed solarium
in which we rise to greet them has no light.

The news we bring them, common, reassuring,
drenched with the cheerful idiocy of noon,
cannot compete with what they have to tell
of what they saw through cracks in the ogre's oven.

And we draw back. The snowy someone says,
Don't mind their talk, they are disturbed today!

OLD MEN WITH STICKS

Old men walking abroad
communicate across distances
by sticks clumping the iron earth of winter,
one, two, answering three,
irregular as the senile pulse
that warms them dimly.

Drawn from the pouch that hangs
like a withered testicle at the belted waist,
pearls without luster are passed without passion
      amongst them;
the dim but enduring stones of hatred
are trafficked amongst them by stealth.

And youth from his lover
draws apart in shame,
looks down and covers
the luster of his nudity,
coughs and cannot return the beloved look.

The ancients, the ancients are walking
aimlessly the dim country.
The moon is a falcon, hooded;
there will be frost. There will indeed be frost
when the bell of space rings
with only withered sticks clumping winter's
      iron earth dully.

ORPHEUS DESCENDING

I

They say that the gold of the under kingdom weighs so
that heads cannot lift beneath the weight of their crowns,
hands cannot lift under jewels,
braceleted arms do not have the strength to beckon.

How could a girl with a wounded foot move through it?

They say that the atmosphere of that kingdom is suffocatingly
    weighted by dust of rubies,
antiquity's dust that comes from the rubbing together of
    jewel and metal, gradual, endless,
a weight that can never be lifted . . .

How could a shell with a quiver of strings break through it?

They say that no light exists in it, but now and again
there is the anguished convulsion of dark into lesser dark,
exposing momently, dimly,
the court's eternal session, nearly immobile,
the courtiers crushed by the golden weight of their robes,
the ladies unable to breathe beneath the weight of their
    blood-dark garlands of roses,
the weight of their eyelids permitting them barely to open.

Orpheus, how could her wounded foot move through it?

II

It is all very well to remember the wonders that you have
    performed in the upper kingdom,
the chasm and forest made responsively vocal,
the course of a river altered as an arm alters when it is bent
    at the elbow,
the moments made to continue by the sweet vibrancy of a
    string pressed by a finger . . .

But those were natural wonders compared to what you essay
    in the under kingdom
and it will not be completed,
no, it will not be completed,

for you must learn, even you, what we have learned,
that some things are marked by their nature to be not
    completed
but only longed for and sought for a while and abandoned.

And you must learn, even you, what we have learned,
the passion there is for declivity in this world,
the impulse to fall that follows a rising fountain.

Now Orpheus, crawl, O shamefaced fugitive, crawl
back under the crumbling broken wall of yourself,
for you are not stars, sky-set in the shape of a lyre,
but the dust of those who have been dismembered by Furies!

PULSE

The tears that pass, becoming
our estate,

the well-intended counsel
wait and wait!

Opacity that crept
upon the eye,

the hot mouth, arch of want,
grown salty dry,

the rooted tongue that copied
the free lark,

the tired neurosis that
still never stops,

and I, and you,
and all foxlike men,

and all hunted men,

and only for one moment,
now and then,

the fierce encounter at
the broken gate,

the lantern quickly snatched
from hand to hand,

the gasping whisper and
the touch, the spark,

the flush that, for one pulse beat,
lets the land

leap fishlike from the struggling
net of dark!

LAMENT FOR THE MOTHS

A plague has stricken the moths, the moths are dying,
their bodies are flakes of bronze on the carpets lying.
Enemies of the delicate everywhere
have breathed a pestilent mist into the air.

Lament for the velvety moths, for the moths were lovely.
Often their tender thoughts, for they thought of me,
eased the neurotic ills that haunt the day.
Now an invisible evil takes them away.

I move through the shadowy rooms, I cannot be still,
I must find where the treacherous killer is concealed.
Feverishly I search and still they fall
as fragile as ashes broken against a wall.

Now that the plague has taken the moths away,
who will be cooler than curtains against the day,
who will come early and softly to ease my lot
as I move through the shadowy rooms with a troubled heart?

Give them, O mother of moths and mother of men,
strength to enter the heavy world again,
for delicate were the moths and badly wanted
here in a world by mammoth figures haunted!

THE ANGELS OF FRUCTIFICATION

There at the center,
solidly planted and passively undergoing a final inspection,
waited the five nude angels of fructification.

Their loamy bellies,
containing freshets and bluets and fluctuant little cloud
     masses,
invisible bells and wires too cunning to measure,
and sockets and pockets to fit them for sexual pleasure,
revolved and revolved with an artfully smooth precision.

A singular hush, for dead lips blow no bugles,
accompanied this half-hour preliminary.

(Here was a place where violence left no debris
and no disaster could interrupt a schedule.)

The troubled Lieutenant stood at the spot marked X.

The troubled Lieutenant remarked, The trouble with all
our technological progress is that it has made
the maker no longer the master.

He watched with a mute concern
and suffered acute heartburn as the headless inspectors,
trusting to finger perception, felt of the flanks
and the warm and rubbery buttocks and of the breasts
whose nipples secreted a sugary bead of moisture
and of the loins whose lips would utter aliveness
after a while, when the passage had been completed.

He shook his head as the headless men stamped approval
on each of the angels at the base of the spine, and set them up
on the motionless belt conveyor.

The Entrance of Azure,
camouflaged to perfection, was noiselessly raised
and the angels started their progress, their birthward march
on the earthward arch of a rainbow.

Each of them made
her individual splendor
                              as she appeared
in the peacefulness of ether.
                              The birds from her vast
umbilicus were released, the torrents of swallows,
the May birds yellow as butter —
and each serenely buttered her puffed-up cheeks
with a childlike smile
and opened her pudgy pink palms on pink tissue paper,
lacily fluted and frilled,
for caps and aprons with French phrase books in the pockets
and cinnamon red hearts to sweeten their fluttering
      tongue-tips.

One thing only
might have incurred suspicion.
The one in the rear
was shinier than the others, and while they purred
like monstrous, innocent kittens,
she, like a serpent, hissed and dripped blue spittle.

And still, ostensibly,
the descent was triumphant.

33

Trumpets declared the approach of the bridal party.

The snowy plateau
of the Andes loomed much closer;
the burning Himalayas lunged their bellies upwards,
longing to plunge in the cooling smother of heaven.

Still obscured by glistening exhalations,
the angels of fructification had now begun
to meet the tumescent phallus of the sun.
Vastly the wheels of the earth sang *Allelulia!*
And the seven foaming oceans bellowed *Oh!*

THE INTERIOR OF THE POCKET

It will not be necessary for you to look very far for the boy.
You will probably find him standing close to where you last
    saw him,
his attitude changed only slightly, his left hand removed
from the relatively austere pocket of the blue jacket
and thrust now into the more companionable pocket of the
    gray pants
so that the glazed material is drawn tight
over the rather surprisingly tenderly sculptured thigh . . .

The interior of the pocket is dark as the dark room he longs to
    sleep in;
it is dark as obliteration of something deeper than sense,
but in it the hot white hand of the boy is closed on itself
with a betrayal of tension his eyes have refused to betray.

for his eyes have not betrayed him. They are somewhat softer
    than blue
and they stay with the afternoon that fades about him, they
    take its color,
they even fade with its color as pieces of sky or water . . .
They show what nakedness is when a thing is truly naked,
and by the very completeness of its exposure is covered up,
when nothing being not seen makes nothing seen . . .

But while you watch him from your respectful distance,
as though he were an experiment in a glass, held over a flame,
about to change, to darken in color or cloud,
a motion occurs under the pocket's dark cover:

the hot white fingers unclose, they come unknotted and they
    extend
slightly sidewise, to offer again their gesture of reassurance
to that part of him, crestfallen, on which he depends
for the dark room he longs to sleep in,

the way small animals nudge one another at night,
as though to whisper, *We're close! There is still no danger!*

THOSE WHO IGNORE THE
APPROPRIATE TIME OF THEIR GOING

I

Those who ignore the appropriate time of their going
  are the most valiant explorers,
going into a country that no one is meant to go into,
the time coming after that isn't meant to come after.

  In the winter of cities
the chalk-drawn sign of the fish, jaws agape on huge
  tongueless outcry
   of suffocation
burns over their white iron beds and gradually brightens,
  casting violent light on them.

  Toward morning, often,
a change occurs in the chemistry of their blood,
  a whitening occurs;

promontories of bone are chalk-marked: to be fractured.
  Blunt instruments cut open
their abdominal cavities, marked: to be stuffed
   with burning sawdust before morning.
  Often, in numbered cubicles,
in the solitude of huge dormitories, ghostly footsteps approach
  them.

  The sister of Rimbaud,
like a white bird, snow-blinded, wanders among the multitude
  of the unsleeping
bearing a warm teacup of a brew from the seeds of the poppy,

rushes, breathless, and kneels
once more to implore them to accept absolution and to be
    sweetly enfolded
        in the blue robe of Mary.

        Clock-tower bells,
        flights of birds,
soften even a city as fierce as Marseilles, and sentiment
        is the drunkenness of pity . . .

        Often, toward morning,
their respiration quickens. Violets are exchanged
between their unlidded eyes and the folds of their disordered
    bedclothes.

        Drawn window blinds
release to the late-watching street
a luster softer than the pearls of a mother.

II

Those that go on through time not meant to admit them
        are the most valiant explorers,
twisting crabwise on their bellies under crisscross barbed wire
    frontiers,
        constantly higher, into more breathless country,
        onto vast snowy plateaus.

Stunted men with fierce dogs rush toward them, firing above
    them to halt them.

Under the falsely pitying corona of light before dawn in high
    country,
they rise erect with the rigid pride of the hopeless
to hold forth hopelessly forged documents, passport photos
    that bear them
        no present resemblance,
and are told to go on, continuing being their glory . . .

        •   •   •

In summer the number is taken away from their door and
    their bed grows double,
        making more room for less slumber.
    As drunken bed partners,
they are incomparably passive and unresponding.
You almost believe they are sleeping until,
        without turning to tell you,
they tell you to go, as gently and simply as they had told you
    to enter.
        (Practices,
            never abandoned,
hold their youth in such thin fingers that tremble!)

III

Longer, much longer than anyone else you know they keep
    the same phone number
        and will answer, if called,
in faraway seashell voices that come and go, as full of distance
        as if they had stayed alone and unmoved
in the torrent that swept you from them farther than far;
        even as though

they offered their soft responses from the same autumn-
    blowing streetcorner
        where you last saw them,
        perhaps still wrapped
in that imperishable military topcoat, spattered so oddly
        with indelible faint blue stains
as though Doom's Partner, whom you've divided between
    you, times without number,
        in one of his brief, gleeful outbursts
inspired by the shock of bar's closing and rude expulsion
        into sea-blowing street,
had one time hurled a fistful of violets at their soft, ill bellies,
        so fiercely,
that stains of this tender outrage still remain there.

        The talk?
        Is not what you wanted.
It's full of long pauses, as though they covered the mouthpiece
        from time to time,
to whisper asides to someone whom you don't know who is in
    the room with them,

        and halfway through it
the truth dawns on you, that whom you are calling isn't them
    at all
        nor anything theirs,
but the youth that you were when you knew them, participan
of their sorrows, and faithful to them.

        From that moment on,
the talk is unbearably awkward. You hang up, forever!
— but gently, gently, folding a bandage over the mouth of a
    wound
that you've observed to be mortal, theirs and your own . . .

       Of course some later summer,
one of that inexhaustible number of later summers that time
    enfolds
to release in languid succession from her geisha-girl sleeve,

         you pass by chance by taxi by where
they once lived, and, oh, wonder
      of all most improbable wonders!
— the brownstone front in which was their cold-water flat
has gone like the tent of an arab,
      and in its place
      now rises most serenely
one of those tall, tall, arrowy slender all steel and glass
    constructions
that cry so high of sky's splendor at all fair daybreaks,
being almost sky, too, almost the lightest part of it,
      and you think, Surely somewhere,
      in language rarer than Sanskrit,
on this fair monolith raised in praise and place of their passion,
      must be graven:
their names and birthdates, precedent to the distinct but short,
    scared dash
      meaning: *Still not gone!*

PHOTOGRAPH AND PEARLS

When I think of how the light touches him,
no more flatteringly in the photograph on his mother's
      mantel
than I have seen it upon his living face
in the glass-rooms of pool and gymnasium where
      I first knew him,

I almost believe, for a moment, in his well-ordered life
that once crossed mine, perpendicularly.
I catch myself, for a split second, persuaded
that it might after all have been somewhat more satisfactory,
finally, not to have torn with such unmannerly hunger
at the coarse fibres of experience
but to have accepted, as he did,
the pacifying dominion of a mother's pearls,
her simplicity and her decorum,
half in and half out of a world where the heart explodes
      momently
with outrageous demands. . . .

But his mother has now returned with the latest and last
      of his letters,
franked by the Navy, seven pages long,
mailed from one of those islands where Paul Gauguin
      died painting
the formalized, purified images of the lust that diseased him.
And I am led to wonder, under the breath of my polite
      attention,
whether or not anybody, half or wholly unclothed,
      golden or brown,

had ever disturbed in the least
his elegant mother's dominion of pearls, to ask myself
if possibly somewhere, craftily concealed between
    the lines
of the seven long pages
may not be half a sentence of something that mothers
    aren't told.

But it is five-thirty, and I am worn out with smiling.
The light is the color of his still
almost too painfully clearly remembered narrow blond head,
and I rise, with a smile of exhaustion, to tell his mother
    goodbye.

THE COMFORTER AND THE BETRAYER

The animal is the comforter and the betrayer,
for he has never seceded altogether from the kingdom of dark,
that perpetual opposite of the state you live in.
He's kept that shadow with him as a part of his being,
bearing it with him contentedly, trustfully,
never glancing back at it, knowing it's there.

Your stolen firelight, that lighted circle you crouch in,
is what he distrusts and shrinks from,
believing it should have been left
an uncontested mystery of the gods.

But his longings are still so familiar that you
mistake them for yours, obliging them continually,
        unthinkingly,
and being only a bit disconcerted, at times,
by the chance discovery
that they are no longer so entirely your own
that their satisfaction appeases all of your heart,
no more entirely your own than his phosphorescent night eyes
are the eyes with which you will face each day's
bland reassurance of a simple existence continued
among your kind. But the animal is

Not only your betrayer but also your comforter.
Since he is faithfully waiting for your return to him
when you have nothing else to return to.
When you return to him
(waiting a little outside the firelight he's never trusted),
he will lick the sensitive hollow of your throat

till it stops painfully throbbing,
he will lick the tips of your fingers with his slow,
        knowing tongue,
so giving you comfort,

While behind him, on the other side of his dishonestly
        sheltering,
quickly but easily panting, treacherous, warm flank

Is your natural destroyer whom he has always known
        to be there,
the dark that he has brought with him. Trust
this betrayer. He is your only comfort.

Part II
THE SUMMER BELVEDERE

THE SUMMER BELVEDERE

I

Such icy wounds the city people bear
beneath brown coats enveloping withered members!

I do not want to know of mutilations

nor witness the long-drawn evening debarkation
of warm and liquid cargoes in torn wrappings
the ships of mercy carry back from war.

We live on cliffs above such moaning waters!

Our eyeballs are starred by the vision of burning cities,
our eardrums shattered by cannon.
A blast of the dying,
a thunder of people who cannot catch their breath

is caught in the mortar and molded into the walls.

And I, obsessed with a dread of things corroded,
of rasping faucets, of channels that labor to flow,
have no desire to know of morbid tissues,
of cells that begin prodigiously to flower.

There is an hour in which disease will be known
as more than occasion for some dim relative's sorrow.
But still the watcher within my soundless country
assures the pendulum duties of the heart
and asks no reason but keeps a faithful watch

as I keep mine from the height of the belvedere!

And though no eyrie is sacred to wind entirely,
a wall of twigs can build a kind of summer.

II

I asked my kindest friend to guard my sleep.

I said to him, Give me the motionless thicket of summer,
the velvety cul-de-sac, and quiet the drummer.

I said to him, Brush my forehead with a feather,
not with an eagle's feather, nor with a sparrow's,
but with the shadowy feather of an owl.

I said to him, Come to me dressed in a cloak and a cowl,
and bearing a candle whose flame is very still.

Our belvedere looks over a brambly hill.

I said to him, Give me the cool white kernel of summer,
the windless terminal of it, and calm the drummer!

I said to him, Tell the drummer
the rebels have crossed the river and no one is here
but John with the broken drumstick and half-wit Peg
who shot spitballs at the moon from the belvedere.

Tell the feverish drummer no man is here.
But what if he doesn't believe me?
                              Give him proof!
For there is no lie that contains no part of truth.

And then, with the sort of courage that comes with fever,
the body becoming sticks that blossom with flame,
the flame for a while obscuring what it consumes,
I twisted and craned to peer in the loftier room —

I saw the visitor there, and him I knew
as my waiting ghost.

The belvedere was blue.

III

I said to my kindest friend, The time has come
to hold what is agitated and make it still.

I said to him, Fold your hands upon the drum.

Permit no kind of sudden or sharp disturbance
but move about you constantly, keeping the guard
with fingers whose touch is narcotic, brushing the walls
to quiet the shuddering in them,
drawing your sleeves across the hostile mirrors
and cupping your palms to breathe upon the glass.

After a while anxiety will pass.

The time has come, I said, for purification.

Rub out the lewd inscriptions on the walls,
remove the prisoners' names and maledictions,
for lack of faith has left impurities here,

and whisper faith to the summer belvedere.

Draw back the kites of hysteria from the sky,
those struggling fish draw back from their breathless pool,
and whisper assurances cool
to the watchful corners, and whisper sleep and sleep
along the treads of the stairs, and up the stair well,

clear to the belvedere, yes, clear up there, where giggling John
stood up in his onionskin of adolescence
to shoot spitballs at the moon from the captain's walk.

And then, at the last, he said, *What shall I do?*
The sweetest of treasons, I told him. Lean toward my
      listening ear
and whisper the long word to me,
the longest of all words to me,
the word that divides the sky from the belvedere.

CORTEGE

I

Cold, cold, cold
was the merciless blood of your father.

By the halo of his breath
your mother knew him;

by January she knew him,
and dreaded the knowledge.

His winter breath
made tears impossible for her.

glazed the air in the kitchen,
dulled the knife,

crusted with ice the milk jug,
soured the butter,

gave fever to all iron objects
and clenched at her throat,

making speech impossible for her.

She passed him and crept sidewise
down the stairs,

loathing the touch
of the doorknob he had clasped.

hating the napkin
he had used at the table.

The children bolted their food
and played outdoors in winter.

Hopscotch took them
blocks away from their father.

Nowhere was ease
but watchfulness in all corners.

The parlor was uncomfortable as the cellar,
the attic was filled with rafts of legal papers,

testimony at lawsuits
stuffed the pillows,

dawn was judicial
and noon made confiscations.

Evening hunched
and hawked on the roof like a jury.

II

The lawyer's house
was always in death's country.

A death was coming.
The minister knew it was coming.

The shroud was cut
before the doctor was summoned.

Winter ached
in the sewing-women's knuckles.

Your mother knew it.
Familiar and loveless knowledge

withered her running heart
and gave it fever.

Arthritis twisted her.
Vivid roses

her blanched face wore in death,
the borrowed plumage of a wealthy cousin . . .

　　·　　　·　　　·

The funeral cortege,
through the financial district,

among the childlike
images of the park

and into the banker's
and brewer's dream of the suburbs

bore with pomp
a woman dead on Monday.

The rumps and nostrils
of horses steamed and frosted.

A mist hung on
the propriety of mourners,

but whisky would hearten
the sentiments felt incumbent

and give unto death
the homage of business partners.

Your father's breath
made tears impossible for you.

It clenched at your throat,
it froze upon your eyelids.

And on that morning —
precociously — for always —

you lost belief
in everything but loss,

gave credence only to doubt,
and began even then,

as though it were always intended,
to form in your heart

the cortege of future betrayals —

the loveless acts
of crude and familiar knowledge.

EVERYMAN

I went to the house of Everyman,
I found his woman there.
I asked her, Where is Everyman?
She said, His home is air.

I asked her, then, What is he like?
She said, No woman knows.
He moaned a little as he crept
beneath my linen clothes.

He lay upon me as a bird,
she said with half disdain.
Why, in the hurry of his wings
he scarcely spoke my name!

And when he left you, did you grieve?
Oh, no, I scarcely knew ...
She rose, and to the window moved,
indolent and huge ...

Then all at once her body broke
in two parts, like a stone,
and as the savage bird escaped,
It's Everyman, she moaned.

PART OF A HERO

I don't suppose that he will be able to build these fires much
    longer
as part of himself must burn like a match struck to light them,

and yet I continue to see him every morning
collecting dry sticks for his tiny conflagration.
And when it is lighted, he crouches before it and shivers,
humming a single, thin note that comes and goes
as though he moved in long, irregular circles, a mournful song
that comes from a shivering monkey, a monkey
not of the tropics but of the poles . . .

Still he would seem to suppose poor Tom's a-cold,
or that something he once took for something of God in his
    heart
has only him to warm it, an obligation too sacred
for him to ignore, and so each morning

out he creeps once more to collect and set ablaze
this silly pile of debris
as earnestly as God must have built the sun.

Each fire may be fatal to him, becoming his auto-da-fé,
but if he's aware of this danger,
it doesn't appear to disturb him, it certainly fails
to deter him,

and when that distinguished time comes, the one that's final,
I think we might suitably honor his passing
with a modest but dignified service. I don't suppose

there will be much left to dispose of,
a handful of powder, bluish and very dark,
and light on the palm as the dropping of a sparrow.

Still, as he goes, as the sable-plumed wind removes him
with that mechanical mourning sound of air's motion,
I will remark to myself, He has gone beyond us.
I may even feel a touch of his exaltation.

And though I may not in the least understand for what reason
he made his choice, or thought it incumbent upon him,
this much will be clear as any of his lost mornings,
that he did own one essential part of a hero,

the idea of life as a nothing-witholding submission of self to
    flame.

DESCENT

It was a steep hill that you went down, calling back to me,
saying that you would be only a little while.
I waited longer than that.
The thin-blooded grass of the hill continued to stir in the wind
and the wind grew colder.

I looked across the deep valley.
I saw that the sun was yellow as lemon upon the dark pines,
but elsewhere pools of cool shadow like stains of dark water
crept gradually onto the hill as the sunlight dimmed.

I waited longer. But finally I rose from the grass
and went back down the path by which we had come
and noted, here and there, your footprints pointing upward,
        narrow and light.

SHADOW BOXES

Old ladies' skulls
are collapsible shadow boxes
containing Louise and Cornelius and Esmeralda,

some of them filmy
as dead flies dissolving in water,
but others still vivid,
        mortality fresher upon them,
exposing their wounds, and complaining:
        You had no pity!

Old ladies' hearts
are cynical imitations of living tissue,
        devices which may,
        without any palpable warning,
just at the moment of rising or going to bed
or climbing the steps of verandas or soaking in baths,
        abandon the *vraisemblance*,

evicting Louise and Cornelius and Esmeralda,
turning all petulant nonpaying residents out
        of the comfortable, lukewarm,
watery matrix of love that plots dissolution —
projecting themselves,
as well as those veteran shadows,
        onto a screen
that is further and further removed,
        a screen in the depths
of a theater filling with smoke —
        till the cinema stops.

INTIMATIONS

I do not think that I ought to appear in public
below the shoulders.
                Below the collar bone
I am swathed in bandages already.
I have received no serious wound as yet
but I am expecting several.
A slant of light reminds me of iron lances;
my belly shudders and my loins contract.

A bandage applied in advance is no prevention.
The wound arrives without a cut in the bandage,
mysteriously, in the night, while the paralyzed
      victim is sleeping.
And then they have to admit, Oh yes, he was right;
apparently his anxieties were well founded!

Rolling his eyes above the pallid sheet, he tries to speak.
So dolorous are those eyes, two hackneyed rhymes,
two pitiful little jingles on epic themes . . .

I reach for the white scratch-pad:
They'll come again!
They'll come again and I'll be unprepared!

Oh, yes, I know that you'll leave the night lamp burning
the makeshift pills, like bits of a china rabbit
with on the bottle the doctor's word *everlasting,*

But I have also observed his conniving wink and grin
as he heard through a rubber tube mortality's roar
    in my veins ...

Alone after midnight in a windy house,
an elderly girl poet
twenty years out of fashion,
bewildered among the debris of romantic boasting,

Bore downstairs her familiar snail's shell, bottle and notebook,
and sat and waited and listened
as a spinster for a caller that still fails to come ...

It would have been less lonely if, starting back up,
she had not set the wine bottle down so carefully beside her
on a low step before dying ...

Under the high and singing forever of darkness,
the strumpet DuBarry,
the manlike woman of Arc,
the priest in flames, the burning Savonarola,
all the heretical host of an out-crying disposition cried aloud
or back of the iron mask of silence,

Wait, wait!

Blue is such a delicate piece of paper.

THE DANGEROUS PAINTERS

I

I told him about the galleries upstairs,
the gilt and velour insulation of dangerous painters.
I said, If they let these plunging creations remain
where they sprung from easels, in rooms accessible
to the subjects of them, in barren studios with broken bottles,
with dangling rubber tubes and the sour smell
of materials hugged for warmth, they would be stored fuel
for a massive indignation. The fingers of misshapen bodies
would point them out, and there would be always
the goatlike cry of "Brother!"
                              The cry of "Brother!"
is worse than the shouting of "Fire!", contains more danger.
For centuries now it has been struck out of our language
except for private usage, in soundproof walls.
These paintings, I said, would prove an excitation,
a chance that could startle this fierce, intolerable cry
from those who forgot it, for only in agony
is there recognition! The paintings would be
a kind of formicary, a racial hive
with double streams, those bringing and taking away
the materials of it, the stuff of hunger,
the matrix of human longing that licks with flame
at the flimsy superstructures, the *trompe-l'œil*
expedients have erected.

                    They find it expedient, then,
to keep these paintings here, as if to say,
This madman died on a gold-brocaded bed,

on cloth of gold this torrent of anger moved.
He had no reason, he acted upon caprice, his will was diseased
that prompted the self-mutilation! And all, all, all
felt only a tender chagrin at his dissipations!

Charwomen have swept the debris of his life away.

I told my friend the story of transmutations,
the painting that hung between madness and dealers'
     hagglings,
the ones suspended by tuberculosis above mockery;
I told him of how the painters had had to make
a religion out of endurance that had no patience in it
but only will and only defiance of factors.
And how they had sifted among the webs of profit
into these opulent halls where connoisseurs
accorded them rosy hum of sound through delicate wires
and women's approval who looked at nothing but mirrors.

This is their way, I said. Do you wish to follow?
The young man smiled and said, I would like to meet them!

I looked at him, then, a youth with veins unswollen,
the kind of purity in him that costs so little,
that comes intact at birth and is not depleted
by any irregular happenings to him since. I shook my head.

Their posthumous reputations are much better.
If I could arrange a meeting, you'd be disappointed,
you'd find their ways oblique, their breath not pleasant,
their handclasp loose and humid. Their posthumous
     reputations
are much, much better!

But some, he said, are my contemporaries!

I wondered how much I knew, how much I could tell him
without exhibiting to him my passport photo.

I told him, then, about the living painters.
These men, I said, are quiet and dangerous persons.
When entertained, they are nervous,
you notice the glass stem trembling in their hands;
their eyes assess the value of your jewels.

What do they fit? Not one convenient label.
For safety, labels are given: they grin and wear them,
conscious of panthers springing through their nerves.
Inspect their pictures! Panthers are always springing
out of the frames, lightning and springing tigers,
long cats springing, something is always springing,
barely leashed by the limitations of canvas.

                                        Don't be sure
that canvas will always contain them, don't be trustful
of any names they are given, but look at their work
and know them hungry men and men whose wives
are mutilated by anger. There is the key,
in the outraged look on the faces of their women,
or lank-bodied youths they lead by invisible chains
through public places. Tigers! Tigers springing!
Their subjects are countries beneath the Tropic of Cancer!

They make bad friends: I've never been easy about them
but felt myself always about to be robbed or beaten
or laughed at when I left them.

                                     Once I was stoned

by a company of five merchants. The painters watched
but none of them interfered.
                         One of them finally
carried me to his room. He comforted me five days,
one day of comfort for each of the malefactors.
But on the evening of the fifth merchant's day
he ceased to smile, the pity moved out of his fingers,
he started to paint.
                         It was not good, it was God,
and I could not endure it. I had to go away.

I said to my young friend, Come!
The painters have left their canvases upstairs,
reposing among the gilt and velour insulation.
They have gone to their rumpled beds to sleep,
to void their tubercular sputum and feel the tigers
running the limitless jungles of their nerves.

Revolution only needs good dreamers.

At night they will start, pressing thumbs to their ears,
sensing the imminence of their dream's explosion!

Do you want that?

He smiled and said, I came for no other reason!

    II

I warned him that he would not be satisfied with it.
I told him that he would not come back changed at all,
for injuries are not changes.
I said to him, Keep the white film over your face

and over your eyelids, merciful white vapor.
Keep whiteness about you always, and never touched
except by the blue of the bones at the stretched kneecaps, the
    faint blurred moons of the armpits and the mystery of
    the groin
that is dark with imagination.
                        Do not touch,
I begged, the *peau de chagrin!* It will not let go.
I told him, It never leaves you!
And still his hands appeared to be curving toward it.

I warned him that he would not want it when he had it,
that he would have it in his hand without knowing where to
    put it down,
that he would have to hold it and to continue to hold it
long, long after it had become a burden,
because it would be too tender to lay aside;
that even if for a moment he laid it aside
and turned to wash his hands at the violet basin,
he'd find it trodden upon when he turned back
for troops of people are always driven through
by the odor of burning!
          I said to him, finally, other arguments failing,
Look at me!
             This was a thing I had never dreamed of doing.
It seemed I was born with knowing I had to be covered
as others from birth accept or seek out watchers.
Now, without preparation, without even trials in private,
I had to expose
            the hot bruised flesh underneath
and point out to him
               the delicate mutilations,
               the webs of veins

that had broken from sudden congestion,
                                where feeling had whirled
those tiny dark spools in me!

Now at this point the galleries must have exploded.
A huge ventilation of walls let in the blue
as faint as the voices of wounded, the gilt and velour
tumbled down wrecked floors to the basement
and birds and serpents vivisected the flame!
The paintings were cracked like plaster walls in
        bombardments;
the subjects, freed, unleashed by the dream's explosion,
trooped down spirals or swung from the loose chandeliers;
the painters themselves began to appear in the wreckage,
naked and ugly as apes at a masquerade party,
their limbs entangled in Clytemnestra's web
but holding above them, on the points of their swords,
the myriad heads of beautiful faithless women!

All time cracked and admitted the truthful flowers.

My last glimpse of him was backed against a wall,
his fists like a panicky boxer's whirling in air.

By seven o'clock the communications were blasted;
the traffic, turned back from the suburbs, found also blocked
the streets of the mercantile section. The opposition
was penned near Union Plaza. I turned away
as the fountains began to play on them molten torrents;
it was all one burning, one pure, intolerable burning —
I turned away ...

Black bread of pity the old nurse gave at supper;

she passed it among the quiet and stupefied people
as evening fell with cinders drifting, drifting,
everywhere cinders drifting.
          The spent and purified people
crouched on the pavements, hunched along broken walls,
and were grateful for stillness,
grateful for effortless breathing now that the wind
had begun to freshen the city.
The city slept.

Part III

THE JOCKEYS AT HIALEAH

THE JOCKEYS AT HIALEAH

For J.

I

At night the drawn blinds
        are light blue instead of green
and hydrants galore give issue to much green water,
        tumble and hum
        with sometimes two in a tub,
with white linen towels or white tissue sprinkled with talcum
in whitewashed cottages where the jockeys are paddocked
        five in a row,
        in sight and sound of the depot...

And everywhere back of the innocent silk of the blinds
in the shotgun cottages, scented with Florida water,
        the hoptoads devote some intervals to the comics,
absorbing the prat-fall with the cosmic projectile,
the villainous domino with the leopard-skin drawers...

But a listener hears,
        if he is expectant and still,
the infinitesimal tick of filaments in light bulbs
        springing out of position,
        fifty-watt Mazdas giving up steady white ghosts.

And after long intervals — talk,
        subdued exclamations!
But couldn't distinguish surprise from indignation,
        quit from *will you?*

Smelling hot oranges in the Loop of Chicago...

The Loop is the way the crow flies
between kids' giggles and lighthearted cohabitation,
between jam sessions and bedrooms at the Blackstone
   (with light bulbs that swing delightedly as you do,
   somewhere between archdeacons and the Voodoo!)

But Electric Avenue stops for NoooooBODY! — who doesn't
  believe
one number comes twice in two throws,
   or thinks God's ignorant of the chance He's taking!

  II

The Sunshine Special has deposited you under skies of pink
  tissue paper
which little girls' scissors will cut into gap-toothed grins and
  triangular eyes.
The cutout sections, looped over telephone wires, will be
  irritably
brushed aside in the rush for entrances.

And you will stop short, coming out of the railroad depot
   thinking you heard your name called,
which is thought-transference, because —
   the face of your love is chalk-white!
    She has taken poison.
The fire department has been called out to revive her.

Her dresses collected grass stains after soft-drink parlors,
and her brother's picture's
a sailor between Hula girls in Honolulu,
framed in forget-me-nots on the ivory bureau.

Her scent is from Liggett's, in half-ounce bottles, the colors
of what the Mexicans call *refrescos y helados*,
vended between the deaths of bulls on Sundays.

She dies likewise eight times between *sol y sombra*
and is hauled by a team of horses across an arena,
but eight times revives and comes back plunging again,
to meet your *banderillos* with bloodshot eyes.

Her hands are like ice and she has called for you twice!

But at five o'clock in the Dutch-blue afternoon,
she is out of danger and you are out of Miami
with all the free pussy there is in a land of plenty!

      Ah, but your silver victrola,
which talked of your losses before it was also lost,
which grieved for your grief before it was also grieved for —
      heavy, heavy hangs over your head and your heart,
and whom will you meet on San Juan de Latrene to redeem it?

    III

Any how now we stopped at a hoptoad's heaven,
one scrub pine and clean sheets without any questions,

radios numbered as blackbirds in the king's pie!

Something all the time going on in the place —
        stud in the parlor,
            pinochle on the back porch,

something suspiciously humming and rattling upstairs,
      which Daisy explained
      was a kind of electric contrivance
for curing inquisitive cats of their bad habits . . .

But to believe in luxury isn't necessarily nor even probably
      to lack dynamism,
and lots of babies who've never been properly weaned from
      Hotel Statler room service
can still make sing, or make like magnificent singing,
      canaries in bedsprings,
being wired to transmit equally well as to receive
        currents of that blue stuff
          which is come of creation,
the doves of Aphrodite's or anyone's car!

IV

The sun makes up with them after a silly quarrel.
Under the feigned and profaned look of magazine cuties,
      Meridians BOOMED!
         Coo-coo!
         Shag ass to breakfast!

The situation involves a poppy kimono, intermittently opened
      to cool off
Bob —

but more of them know than you would suspect of knowing
the *faute-de-mieux* convenience . . .

      And evening makes a difference in a place.

Somebody buffs his shoes with a steady buff.
Somebody looks in a chiffonier for something
which turns out not to be there,
 or if it is there, is not the right color or size,
 or proves in some other respect an unpleasant
  surprise.
Somebody thinks he is quicker than somebody's buddy who's
 bigger
  and heigh-ho,
  off they both go
   in the Black Maria!

Yes, evening makes a difference in a place
  much like a drunkard's poem before his blonde
calls — Waiter! Check! We're leaving...
Bibulous sonnet, too deep for appreciation —

  and bed's ENORMOUS!
  Big as a fire truck, rockets us to slumber,
hanging on brass-hinged ladders with faraway eyes...

RECUERDO

1. *The Bloodless Violets*

And he remembered the death of his grandmother
whose hands were accustomed to draw white curtains about
    him
before he moved to Electric Avenue...

In childhood's spectrum of violence, she remained pale,
a drift of linen among tall, sunny chambers.

It was not ordained by God, nor any minister of Him,
that time should be caught in the withered crook of her elbow
or that she who would not
                           give injury to birds,
had nevertheless been called upon to carry
a cage full of swallows into an evil guest chamber

because her hands,
         the knuckles of which were arthritic,
         finger tips numbed by winter,
could not disengage
         the long-ago hairpin twisted about the cage door...

But Spring's first almost bloodless violets were removed
from the washing machine in the basement,
         making it plain
         why such a contagion of languor,
           brought indoors with the laundry,
made visitors yawn.

Possibly also explaining why slumber's mischievous
    matchmaking
had put him to bed with young witches,
        indistinct beings anonymous of gender,
        some of them only a hollowness fastened upon his
            groin
and drawing, drawing,
        the jelly out of his bones and leaving him only,
            finally,
                tenderly,
                    coldly —
the damp initial of Eros.

2. *Episode*

And then the long, long peltering schools of rain!

        Ozzie, the black nurse,
           tussles with the awnings,
               a peppery kind of battle
in which she is worsted.
               — Lightning,
                   her starched white skirt,
is yanked across heaven!
    Aw, God, Mizz Williams!
    — horse liniment stung her,
And in the morning,
                a telephone pole in our attic,
        slippery, blanched —
        A Mississippi tornado!

3. *The Paper Lantern*

My sister was quicker at everything than I.

At five she could say the multiplication tables
      with barely a pause for breath,
      while I was employed
with frames of colored beads in Kindy Garden.

At eight she could play
                  Idillio and The Scarf Dance
while I was chopping at scales and exercises.

At fifteen my sister
               no longer waited for me,
impatiently at the White Star Pharmacy corner
      but plunged headlong
      into the discovery, Love!

Then vanished completely —

for love's explosion, defined as early madness,
consumingly shone in her transparent heart for a season
and burned it out, a tissue-paper lantern!

          — torn from a string!
          — tumbled across a pavilion!

flickering three times, almost seeming to cry ...
My sister was quicker at everything than I.

THE LEGEND

I

They built a new temple where the old had fallen
in the long and terrible days of Indian summer.
Their eyes in their skulls
    admitted no sensible light.
They walked with hands pressed to their mouths,
    observing a law of silence
        while the crossed blades shone
            wicked and jewel-like
in atmosphere that shook with September heat.

It must have been she that spoke first
the damned thing they were forbidden,
    ugly upon her lips as something which had been
        scrawled
    with a thick black stub of pencil
across a wall . . .

He turned, coughing dryly a little,
as if to stamp out
            with sudden look of denial
that muttering speech.
But it was too late —
    already those flames, tinder-quick,
        the sperm of the goatlike summer
        that ravaged her loins,
had licked up the steep hillside.

Those stunted bushes,
    the ones with the hard red berries,

81

accepted the fire almost as a benediction,
and passed it on,
                    from tree to little tree,
                        from branch to branch,
till silently all the hillside quivered with light.

II

And still he would not look at her.

Her head was a thick chunk of amber
    the light shone through,
        transformed from blocks to spear points.

Her limbs divided,
    spread indolently fanwise,
        the wings of a tired butterfly ...

        Her eyes dropped downward, mocking,
        to where his body had raised
        a part of itself
        like a child's hand raised
        to ask to answer a question.

        Adam! Adam!

And now the whole afternoon
had hardened into a block of transparent amber,
    no longer water,
        difficult to wade through,
but something that locked
    all movement absolutely ...

Yes, he admitted.
        the tongue in his mouth like cotton,
I want to touch you!

The crossed blades shifted,
        the wind blew south, and forever
the birds, like ashes, lifted
        away from that hot center —

but they, being lost,
        could not observe an omen —
        they knew only
the hot, quick arrow of love
        while metals clashed,
                a battle of angels above them,
and thunder — and storm!

LIFE STORY

After you've been to bed together for the first time,
without the advantage or disadvantage of any prior
    acquaintance,
the other party very often says to you,
Tell me about yourself, I want to know all about you,
what's your story? And you think maybe they really and
    truly do

sincerely want to know your life story, and so you light up
a cigarette and begin to tell it to them, the two of you
lying together in completely relaxed positions
like a pair of rag dolls a bored child dropped on a bed.

You tell them your story, or as much of your story
as time or a fair degree of prudence allows, and they say,
    Oh, oh, oh, oh, oh,
each time a little more faintly, until the oh
is just an audible breath, and then of course

there's some interruption. Slow room service comes up
with a bowl of melting ice cubes, or one of you rises to pee
and gaze at himself with mild astonishment in the bathroom
    mirror.
And then, the first thing you know, before you've had time
to pick up where you left off with your enthralling life story,
they're telling you *their* life story, exactly as they'd intended
    to all along,

and you're saying, Oh, oh, oh, oh, oh,
each time a little more faintly, the vowel at last becoming
no more than an audible sigh,

as the elevator, halfway down the corridor and a turn to
     the left,
draws one last, long, deep breath of exhaustion
and stops breathing forever. Then?

Well, one of you falls asleep
and the other one does likewise with a lighted cigarette
     in his mouth,
and that's how people burn to death in hotel rooms.

THE MAN IN THE DINING CAR

Seated motionless among sliding landscapes
humped or flattened beneath their incongruous load
of agrarian impedimenta,
       the man in the dining car
       ignored Wyoming,
was conscious only of what he wished to forget,
which clung to him all the closer because of his wanting
   to lose it.

Always when a partition lifted another one closed.

He was locked inside the airless box of his skull
       with only the perceptual members of his body,
       such as the eyes, the mouth, the fingers,
       and very briefly, the sex,
affording him some measure of escape.

Yes, he grew restive against confinement,
       bought a one-way ticket to another place,
       changed his name,
       enlarged his list of acquaintances
       with new faces
disappointingly similar to those before.

Now in the railroad diner
       he waited for motion
       to lift a stone from his breast.
But the stone kept traveling with him,
       got on the train at Manhattan, still remained at
       Chicago,

        still remained at St. Paul,
        still remained at Cheyenne,
appeared, in fact, to be making a transcontinental excursion.

He fingered his vest,
        took the watch out of his pocket,
        removed the chain,
        unfastened the top three buttons;
the weight remained.

What he carried with him was an invisible ballast.

He wondered how he would feel without it:
        very light? Immaterial even?
Yes, perhaps without it
        railway transportation would not be necessary at all;
        specific gravity would be lost altogether.

Metallic glimmerings
        in the vast noon sun above Wyoming
        would mark his aerial passage.

A subtle, complacent hum in the brilliant atmosphere
        would barely announce him to strangers.

But now, in the meantime, still
        with the bouillon cup before him containing a fine
        and colorless sediment of beef and grain,

he practiced the Yogi method
        of muscular relaxation,
        making himself slacken out like a broken string.

But still his mouth remained compressed and dry
        while his vision kept on catching
        the senseless succession of scudding telegraph poles.

THE DEATH EMBRACE

I

From distance that drew me closer it seemed I could hear
the sound of machines in motion,
of huge cylindrical objects that gleamed with oil.

Not only the sound but also the vision grew clearer.

Now everything moved
with a kind of ecstatic precision;
no surface but sheer, no socket but fitted the gear
with a frictionless rhythm.

The men in blue,
mechanical, mindless puppets,
all of one height, identical in their appearance,
had cotton wads stuffed in their ears to protect their eardrums
against that continual thunder;
their eyes were guarded by goggles they had to wipe clean
of oil spattered on them.
The great wheels spat
like cats, with incredible malice;
the hands wore gloves, for what they touched was electric.
The glare was intense, the heat eternal, terrific.
If some unit erred
in performance of its certain function,
auxiliary units were instantly set in motion;
the change so quick you would not know it occurred.

II

At last came a time when the clock rang loudly above them;
then on the balcony, over the scene of their labor,
the foreman advanced with a gas mask over his features.

He glanced at his watch and then again at the clock
and he cleared his throat.

The men in blue were attentive, they gave the salute;
the foreman returned it to them.

He shouted in some strange language a certain command.

Instantly, then, adjustments were made beneath him;
the men in blue
drew levers, turned wheels, pressed buttons.

Then everything bulged
in a kind of a burning white vapor.

With cries like birds'
the blue men scattered before it
to stations determined by X's marked on a chart.

After a moment the vapor was cleared away.

Then those who watched, from the galleries high above,
observed with regret that was tempered by admiration
that none of the men who had labored in blue were living.

Then long, slow sighs of solemn and sad approbation,
like moist white flowers whose petals ballooned in the air,

floated down through the room
and settled about those bodies which did not move.

The foreman advanced, with gas mask over his face,
to read an announcement.
These men, he said, *have liquidated themselves
for the good of the State!*
Oh, then, what applause, what a ringing of bells was started!

Down spiral stairways that were draped with imperial purple
the spectators filed
and out, then, into the street,
with the foreman before them, receiving loud acclamations,
to form a parade, to march through an *arc de triomphe*
in the great throbbing heart of the marvelous capital city!

III

A long way off
I heard those machines in motion,
the dull, muffled turning
of huge cylindrical objects immersed in oil.

And this that I heard was counterpoint to our passion.

But you were near, and I told you nothing about it,
for you were small,
and the turning wheels were tremendous...

I think of it now and am glad that I never told you

for where you were
the sound was diminished to music,
a faint, faint hum, mistakable for a spinet...

The light was dim, and there was no terror in it.

The light was dim

and there was no terror in it.

THE CHRISTUS
OF GUADALAJARA

I

The Christus of Guadalajara
waits for the scarlet tomorrow.
His womanish fingers twitch
at a silvery crucifix
and ashes of roses fall
on His sandals in the hall.
His nakedness, sweet with musk
and pale as the mother of pearl
that enveloped a stainless world,
is stretched out cool in the dusk,
ready to be put on
the moment that He is born.

II

Swallows in circles bewildered
whirl from the dark iron bells,
and over the square the *gitana*
cannot work her spells.
The room is shadowy, tall,
and filled with the murmur of rain.
Indians crouch in the corners
with moonlike saucers of grain.
The bottles of Lachryma Christi
are stored on the spidery shelves,
and the saints of tomorrow groan
as they flagellate themselves.

III

A stone that covers the stairs
from the dungeon is lifted away
and the Mother of God emerges,
little and patient and gray.
Ignoring the murmurs of comfort,
She kneels to arrange as before
the mothlike garments of Gesu
over the cold stone floor,
kissing the delicate stitches,
tenderly blessing them,
and scattering tears like jewels
over the silken hem.

IV

Time is a long-drawn thunder
of waters under the ground
as high in the vaulted ceiling
the bells are beginning to sound.
The Christus of Guadalajara
cannot wake nor sleep.
The angels hover above Him
To catch His fluttering speech.
He whispers love and love,
the angels answer death,
and the shuddering hush between
is Sancta Maria's breath.

V

The Christus of Guadalajara
turns in His salted sheet.
Into His palms are driven
the nails and into His feet.
O Mother of God, have mercy,
He cries, and if She could
Our Lady would give Her crown
to ransom a drop of His blood.
But alone in Her anguish as He,
La Madrecita has curled
in a lampless corner to bear
Her terrible Rose of the World.

CARROUSEL TUNE

Turn again, turn again, turn once again;
the freaks of the cosmic circus are men.

We are the gooks and geeks of creation;
Believe-It-or-Not is the name of our star.
Each of us here thinks the other is queer
and no one's mistaken since all of us are!

Turn again, turn again, turn once again;
the freaks of the cosmic circus are men.

We sweat and we fume in a four-cornered room
and love is the reason. But what does love do?
It gives willy-nilly to poor silly Billy
the chance to discover what daddy went through.

Turn again, turn again, turn once again;
the freaks of the cosmic circus are men.

We may hum and hop like a musical top
or stop like a clock that's run down,
but why be downhearted, the season's just started,
and new shows are coming to town!

Turn again, turn again, turn once again;
the freaks of the cosmic circus are men.

IRON IS THE WINTER

Iron is the winter, locked upon the south,
locked on the mountains where the springs are fed;
and still our blood is sacred; to the mouth
the tongue of the beloved is holy bread.

Steel is the glacier and the fields of snow
are locked by firs inviolate of sound;
those forests breathe, their giant white nostrils blow
frost on the steeples; quietly sleeps the town.

The frozen heroes whose tremendous wounds
are roses sculptured in the *mer de glace*
slumber as children in blue peaceful rooms,
with lips that smile incredible advice.

Who is the comer that destroys the snow,
whose track appears triangular and vast?
One moment seen, the demon robot's face
explodes from thought the moment he is past.

We hear no warning, yet awake and turn;
infinity cries loudly overhead;
as earth divides, our bodies meet and burn
and in our mouths we take the holy bread.

Part IV
HOOFPRINTS OF A LITTLE HORSE

WHICH IS MY LITTLE BOY?

For Carson McCullers

Which is my little boy, which is he,
Jean qui pleure ou Jean qui rit?

Jean qui rit is my delicate John,
the one with the Chinese slippers on,

whose hobbyhorse in a single bound
carries me back to native ground.

But *Jean qui pleure* is *mysterieux*
with sorrows older than Naishapur,

with all of the stars and all of the moons
mirrored in little silver spoons.

Which is my little boy, which is he,
Jean qui pleure ou Jean qui rit?

LADY, ANEMONE

The body burned away the parting cloth.
    As though a compass hand had pointed north,
he moved!
    Storms, waterfalls, and tall men
move this way —
    tremendous impulse draws them,
not to stay!
        Lady,
            anemone,
                    violet-soft and kissing,
tender scabbard with a fierce blade missing . . .

    You will awake to find a tall man gone,
his north become the morning.
                          Like a tear,
it trembles, hesitates, turns very clear,
illustrious morning, weather of his smile.

    Who brought, enveloped in a rainbow storm,
eleven fingers wanting to be warmed,
    and having warmed them —
                        lifted with a twist
that put you under him at least a mile!

For keepsakes leaving silver on a wrist,
    gold on a finger,
        bruises on your thigh . . .
It's only being tired that makes you cry.

HEAVENLY GRASS

From *Blue Mountain Ballads*

My feet took a walk in heavenly grass.
All day while the sky shone clear as glass.
My feet took a walk in heavenly grass,
All night while the lonesome stars rolled past.
Then my feet come down to walk on earth,
And my mother cried when she give me birth.
Now my feet walk far and my feet walk fast,
But they still got an itch for heavenly grass.
But they still got an itch for heavenly grass.

LONESOME MAN

From *Blue Mountain Ballads*

My chair rock-rocks by the door all day
But nobody ever stops my way,
Nobody ever stops by my way.

My teef chaw-chaw on an old ham bone
An' I do the dishes all alone,
I do the dishes all by my lone.

My feet clop-clop on the hardwood floor
'Cause I won't buy love at the hardware store,
I don't want love from the mercantile store.

Now the clock tick-tocks by my single bed
While the moon looks down at my sleepless head,
While the moon grins down at an ole fool's head.

CABIN

From *Blue Mountain Ballads*

The cabin was cozy and hollyhocks grew
Bright by the door till his whisper crept through.
The sun on the sill was yellow and warm
Till she lifted the latch for a man or a storm.

Now the cabin falls to the winter wind
And the walls cave in where they kissed and sinned.
And the long white rain sweeps clean the room
Like a white-haired witch with a long straw broom!

SUGAR IN THE CANE

From *Blue Mountain Ballads*

I'm red pepper in a shaker,
Bread that's waitin' for the baker.
I'm sweet sugar in the cane,
Never touched except by rain.
If you touched me God save you,
These summer days are hot and blue.

I'm potatoes not yet mashed,
I'm a check that ain't been cashed.
I'm a window with a blind,
Can't see what goes on behind.
If you did, God save your soul!
These winter nights are blue and cold!

KITCHEN DOOR BLUES

My old lady died of a common cold.
She smoked cigars and was ninety years old.
She was thin as paper with the ribs of a kite,
And she flew out the kitchen door one night.

Now I'm no younger 'n the old lady was,
When she lost gravitation, and I smoke cigars.
I feel sort of peaked, an' I look kinda pore,
So for God's sake, lock that kitchen door!

GOLD TOOTH BLUES

Now there's many fool things a woman will do
To catch a man's eye, she'll wear a tight shoe,
She'll wear a light dress and catch a bad cold
And have a tooth pulled for a tooth of gold.

I'm a gold tooth woman with the gold tooth blues
'Cause a gold tooth makes a woman look old!

Now gold in the bank is a wonderful thing,
And a woman looks nice with a nice gold ring,
But, honey, take a tip, and the tip ain't cold,
Your mouth's no place to carry your gold!

I'm a gold tooth woman with the gold tooth blues
'Cause a gold tooth makes a woman look old!

Some late Sunday mawnin' when you're still in the hay
And you want a little lovin', your sweet man'll say,
With a look that'll turn your heart's blood cold,
Woman, that gold tooth makes you look old!

I'm a gold tooth woman with the gold tooth blues
'Cause a gold tooth makes a woman look old!

When your man's out of money and he must have a drink,
He'll sneak up behind you at the kitchen sink,
And before you can holler, I'm telling the truth,
He'll brain you with a black-jack and pull your gold tooth!

I'm a gold tooth woman with the gold tooth blues
'Cause a gold tooth makes a woman look old!

HER HEAD ON THE PILLOW

In the morning I watched her rise
and in the night lie down,
and I swear that her head on the pillow was bright
as Holy Mary's crown;
I swear that her head on the pillow was bright
as Mary's golden crown.

The heart is drawn to a thing so light
and the hand to a thing so warm,
but I swear that I pressed a stone to my heart
when I took the lady by storm;
I swear that I pressed my heart to a stone
when I covered her by storm.

A shadow fell on her face that night
and her hand on the lace of her gown,
but I swear that her head on the pillow was bright
as Holy Mary's crown;
I swear that her head on the pillow was bright,
as Mary's golden crown.

ACROSS THE SPACE

I

Across the space between
a bed and chair
I watch you fade into
the fading air.

Intimate these moments,
dim and warm.
My finger tips could touch
your unsleeved arm

and so release the fire
and brutal shock
suspended in quiet air
and tender watch.

I say I could, and it
may be I will,
but have forborne and am
forbearing still,

for there is something delicate
and rare
drawn tight across the space
from bed to chair.

II

It is delusion that
this quiet could bloom
something that's timeless in
our little room,

for time's not cheated by
a moment's quiet;
the heartbeats echo to
eternal riot.

The cock will crow his fading
stars among;
the lie is only waiting
on the tongue!

But while it waits, I speak not
false to you;
something unspoken in
the room is true;

something that's delicate
and dim and rare
breathes in the space between
a bed and chair.

MY LITTLE ONE

My little one whose tongue is dumb,
whose fingers cannot hold to things,
who is so mercilessly young,
he leaps upon the instant things,

I hold him not. Indeed, who could?
He runs into the burning wood.
Follow, follow if you can!
He will come out grown to a man

and not remember whom he kissed,
who caught him by the slender wrist
and bound him by a tender yoke
which, understanding not, he broke.

THE ISLAND IS
MEMORABLE TO US

The island is memorable to us
as the change of a mirror
or an underground river.

The island loses in going.
It appears to be still.
Half of it, now, is in shadow,

and yet it increases in going,
memorable as the moon's changes.
It makes unnoticed advances

with an appearance of yielding;
it slips through the fingers,
a stone with a milky luster . . .

No, you cannot hold it, it
twists like a woman! Its nights
are memorable to us: the black

rope-straining goat's golden-
eyed gaze at our passings,
the leghorn rooster, white

as a bare body's twisting, the cross
enclosed by the cipher, the night
enclosed by the rose . . .

Oh, heavy our flow
compared to the weight of an island!
For we are the anchored, the island

a constant white gliding!

SAN SEBASTIANO DE SODOMA

How did Saint Sebastian die?
Arrows pierced his throat and thigh
which only knew, before that time,
the dolors of a concubine.

Near above him, hardly over,
hovered his gold martyr's crown.
Even Mary from Her tower
of heaven leaned a little down

and as She leaned, She raised a corner
of a cloud through which to spy.
Sweetly troubled Mary murmured
as She watched the arrows fly.

And as the cup that was profaned
gave up its sweet, intemperate wine,
all the golden bells of heaven
praised an emperor's concubine.

TUESDAY'S CHILD

My brother Jack was wild.
That's frequently the case with Tuesday's child
who has the gift of grace and no gift other —
>> but I
>> have had no lover.

Iron numerals give the address, and the year's
engraved, not written.
>> I was three times bitten,
by frost and a neighbor's dog and a cousin's child —
once felt a touch that burned through my heart's cover
but could not speak nor move away nor turn . . .
>> I have no lover.

My brother Jack was wild
with mistresses who circled him like moons,
>> one black, one gold,
>> one turning early gray,
and while the piper's waiting for his pay
he still will play the most bewitching tunes!
>> But I
>> have had no lover.

My brother Jack is wild.
He watches leaping things and things that fly
and distances that hounds or falcons cover.
>> But I have watched a spider in the sky
that spins gray lace as patiently as I
>> wait for my brother . . .

TOWNS BECOME JEWELS

Towns become jewels
at seven, after sunset,
pearled with lamps,
the arcades lit for pleasure ...

High, high, high
is the night's thin music above them!

Oh, why are they not
as once we believed they were,

incorruptible gems,
true diamonds dropped in water?

MORNINGS ON BOURBON STREET

He knew he would say it. But could he believe it again?

He thought of the innocent mornings on Bourbon Street,
of the sunny courtyard and the iron
lion's head on the door.

He thought of the quality light could not be expected
to have again after rain,

the pigeons and drunkards coming together from under
the same stone arches, to move again in the sun's
faint mumble of benediction with faint surprise.

He thought of the tall iron horseman before the Cabildo,
tipping his hat so gallantly toward old wharves,
the mist of the river beginning to climb about him.

He thought of the rotten-sweet odor the Old Quarter had,
so much like a warning of what he would have to learn.

He thought of belief and the gradual loss of belief
and the piecing together of something like it again.

But, oh, how his blood had almost turned in color
when once, in response to a sudden call from a window,
he stopped on a curbstone and first thought,

Love. Love. Love.

He knew he would say it. But could he believe it again?

He thought of Irene whose body was offered at night
behind the cathedral, whose outspoken pictures were hung
outdoors, in the public square,
as brutal as knuckles smashed into grinning faces.

He thought of the merchant sailor who wrote of the sea,
haltingly, with a huge power locked in a halting tongue —

lost in a tanker off the Florida coast,
the locked and virginal power burned in oil.

He thought of the opulent antique dealers on Royal
whose tables of rosewood gleamed as blood under lamps.

He thought of his friends.

He thought of his lost companions,
of all he had touched and all whose touch he had known.

He wept for remembrance.

But when he had finished weeping, he washed his face,

he smiled at his face in the mirror, preparing to say
to you, whom he was expecting,

Love. Love. Love.

But could he believe it again?

THE LAST WINE

These rooms are public as a place
where strangers come to stay the night;
the court is spacious though bathed in
a curious, oblique gray light.

A bell is rung at every hour
to startle sleeping men awake;
a watchman stationed in the tower
cries pardon for the bell's mistake.

Yet you who take repeated shocks
without too visible dismay
can watch the gilded weathercocks
peck the starry corn away

until along those spiral stairs,
descending from some place apart,
the sightless, smiling watchman bears
the last wine from the master's heart.

THE ROAD

I've traveled this road thirty years,
gone West
        a little too often,
am now past all redemption.

(Sixteen cases of soft-sole slippers,
odd lots, broken merchandise,
prices ranging from three to thirteen dollars.)

I boarded the Pullman at Joplin,
went to the bar,
        gazed reflectively at my reflection,
        rattled the ice in my glass.

I never speak to strangers.

Sometime I think I will ride into St. Louis
on the back of a snow-white ass.
I will pass along Washington Boulevard,
wholesale artery of the Middle West,
through crowds bearing branches of palms
and the cry will go up,
        His Honor!
        His Honor!
        His Honor in the Highest!

I will lay out my samples in the lobby of the Hotel Statler
and afterward I will be brought up before the paunchy pilot,

        crucified on Art Hill, dead and buried.

And on the third day I will rise again from the dead
and break all previous records for cash sales!

Blizzards of ticker tape!
    Goose-pimples all over!
    Aldermen's greetings!
    Oh golly!

LITTLE HORSE

For F. M.

Mignon he was or *mignonette*
avec les yeux plus grands que lui.
My name for him was Little Horse.
I fear he had no name for me.

I came upon him more by plan
than accidents appear to be.
Something started or something stopped
and there I was and there was he.

And then it rained but Little Horse
had brought along his *parapluie.*
Petit cheval it kept quite dry
till he divided it with me.

For it was late and I was lost
when Little Horse enquired of me,
What has a bark but cannot bite?
And I was right. It was a tree.

Mignon he is or *mignonette*
avec les yeux plus grands que lui.
My name for him is Little Horse.
I wish he had a name for me.

DEATH IS HIGH

Death is high;
it is where the exalted things are.
I know, for breathlessness took me
to a five-pointed star.

I was exalted
but not at ease in that space.
Beneath me your breathing face
cried out, Return, Return.

Return, you called while you slept.
And desperately back I crept
against the ascending fall.

It was not easy to crawl
against those unending torrents of light,
all bending one way,

and only your voice calling, Stay!

But my longing was great
to be comforted and warmed
once more by your sleeping form,

to be, for a while, no higher
than where you are,
little room, warm love, humble star!

OLD MEN ARE FOND

Old men are fond
of little certainties.
The mail will arrive
at exactly three-forty-five,
the crossword puzzle will be
in the upper lefthand corner of
page twenty-three.

The weight of a baby,
the length and breadth of a shoe,
the exact amount of a bill
and when it is due,

the place where it happened,
not why, but precisely when.

Old men
are not at all fond
of going beyond

familiar attachments. . . .

They don't want to roam in the gloam or to comb
the future with a fine-tooth comb
too far from home.

No, old men are not at all fond
of going much distance beyond

SHADOW WOOD

I once looked on a young green tree
that shattered darkness where it stood.
The name of it was tenderness
and where it grew was Shadow Wood.

The leaves of it were little hands
that scattered gold that had no weight,
and never dimmed to lesser gold:
it would have held me could I wait.

Somewhere it stays in grace of light
but I've forgotten where it stood,
and once abandoned, never twice
can it be found in Shadow Wood.

For tenderness I would lay down
the weapon that holds death away,
but little words of tenderness
are hard for shadow man to say.

A SEPARATE POEM

I

The day turns holy as though a god moved through it,
wanderingly, unknowing and unknown,
led by the sky as a child is led by its mother.

But the sky of an island is a wandering sky.
It seems bewildered sometimes, it seems bewildered as we are
since the loss of our island.
Oh, yes, we've lost our island.

                                Time took it from us,
snatched it out of our hands as a fresh runner snatches
out of a spent runner's hand
the bit of white cloth to continue.

                           Still
we live on the island, but more as visitors,
than as residents, now.

                         Still we remember
things our island has taught us: how to let the sky go
      (as a bit of white cloth to continue)
and other things of a smaller, more intimate nature.
Our island has been a school in which we were backward
      pupils
but, finally, learning a little, such as:
lies die, but truth doesn't live except in the truth of our island
which is a truth that wanders, led by the sky
as a child is led by its mother, and the sky wanders, too.

II

I dreamed one night without sleeping that when I returned,
that night, to a northern island,
you put on the clothes of a god which was your naked body
and moved from window to window in a room made of
    windows, drawing, closing the curtains, your back
turned to me, showing no sign that you knew that you were
building an island: then came to rest, fleshed
in a god's perfection beside me.
                    Even then,
I knew that to build an island is not to hold it always,
    but longing was so much stronger, yes, even stronger
than the dread of not holding, always.

Perhaps it would have been better if I had touched only
    your hand,
or only leaned over your head and clasped it all the night
    through.
    But longing was so much stronger....:

III

Our travels ranged wide of our island but nowhere nearly
    so far
as our silence now enters the bare and mountainous country
of what cannot be spoken.
                    When we speak to each other
we speak of things that mean nothing of what we meant
    to each other.
                    Small things
gather about us as if to shield our vision from a wide landscape
untouched by the sun and yet blindingly lighted.
                    We say small things to each other

in quiet, tired voices, hoarsened as if by shouting
       across a great distance.
              We say small things to each other carefully, politely,
              such as:
Here's the newspaper, which part of it do you want?
Oh, I don't care, any part but the funnies or ads....

              But under the silence of what we say to each other,
is the much more articulate silence of what we don't say to
       each other,
              a storm of things unspoken,
              coiled, reserved, appointed,
ticking away like a clock attached to a time-bomb:
              crash, fire, demolition

                            wound up in the quietly,
almost tenderly,
              small, familiar things spoken.

       IV

              Do you remember, as I do,
that in the temple of the Emerald Buddha in Bangkok,
              there was, near the entrance,
a table bearing a laughable assortment of western gadgets,
       such as:
              a portable radio called *Zenith*,
              an electric razor called *Sunbeam*,
              an alarm-clock called *Little Ben* that was actually
              ticking?
And as for the Emerald Buddha, both of us thought him
       disconcertingly small,
              not glittering but glazed,

and he was just sitting there to be visited and observed by
    travelers
tired of travel, tourists tired of touring.

It was the long, slow, golden-hazed boat trip
through the canals of Bangkok
that gave us a sense of reverence for something:
the shacks on stilts of bamboo, the ancient women, breasts
    drooping,
bathing their grandsons in the warm tawny water as if
    paying them homage
as loving as it was humble: this, only this,
spoke to us of the limitless range and simplicity of a god, just
this, not the Emerald Buddha in his funnily tacky pavilion....

The water of islands and the sky of islands
are what draw back to us
the visiting god that wanders, unable to speak any language
but that of stillness and radiance outside our windows.

Later, all dims, and nothing is asked past our measure;
the evening of our island
is simple as the question: What shall we have for supper?
and the answer: What would you like for supper?
In voices turned softer by love's exhaustion and hate's.

A true god's image, unless it is drawn by a god,
(and I doubt that they pose for each other)
is better drawn in such quick, light pencil-scratches....